P9-CRD-055

OUTSTANDING AFRICAN AMERICANS

GREAT AFRICAN AMERICANS IN

GOVERNMENT

KAREN DUDLEY

Crabtree Publishing Company

MAY 04
KN

Dedication

This series is dedicated to the African-American men and women who followed their dreams. With courage, faith, and hard work, they overcame obstacles in their lives and went on to excel in their fields. They set standards as some of the best Olympic athletes in the world. They brought innovation to film, jazz, and the arts, and the world is richer for their touch. They became leaders, and through their example encouraged hope and self-reliance. *Outstanding African Americans* is both an acknowledgment of and a tribute to these people.

Project Manager
Lauri Seidlitz

Production Manager
Amanda Howard

Editor
Virginia Mainprize

Copy Editor
Janice Parker

Design
Warren Clark

Layout
Chris Bowerman

Photograph Credits
Cover: Powell photo (Globe: Michael Ferguson), Moseley-Braun photo (U.S. Senate), Chisholm photo (Globe: Neil Heilpern); **Yvonne Braithwaite Burke:** page 15; **Charles L. Blockson Afro-American Collection, Temple University:** page 6; **Globe Photos:** pages 16 (Tommy Noonan), 18 (Neil Heilpern), 21 (Thom Jackson), 23 (Mitchell Levy), 34 (Michael Ferguson), 37 (James M. Kelly), 38 (Lisa Rose), 42 (James Reilly), 45 (Marcel Thomas), 49 (Adam Scull), 55 (Jim Pickerell), 58 (John Barrett), 4, 28; **Reuters/Bettmann:** pages 24 (Mike Theiler), 25 (Jim Bourg), 26 (Scott Olson), 27, 36 (Ira Schwarz), 41 (Shunsuka Akatsuka); **Schomburg Center for Research in Black Culture, New York Public Library:** pages 10, 17, 29, 30; **Urban Archives, Temple University, Philadelphia, Pennsylvania:** pages 9 (International News Photo), 7, 8, 11, 12; **U.S. Senate:** page 22; **UPI/Corbis-Bettmann:** pages 19 (Vince Marino), 35, 43 (Cliff Owen), 39 (Ray Foli), 40 (Joe Mahoney), 44 (Martin Jeong), 46 (Richard Fowlkes), 52 (J.C. Anderson), 5, 13, 14, 20, 31, 32, 33, 61.

Every reasonable effort has been made to trace ownership and to obtain permission to reprint copyright material. The publishers would be pleased to have any errors or omissions brought to their attention so that they may be corrected in subsequent printings.

Published by
Crabtree Publishing Company

350 Fifth Avenue,	360 York Road, R.R. 4	73 Lime Walk
Suite 3308	Niagara-on-the-Lake	Headington
New York, NY	Ontario, Canada	Oxford OX3 7AD
U.S.A. 10018	L0S 1J0	United Kingdom

Copyright © 1997 WEIGL EDUCATIONAL PUBLISHERS LIMITED. All rights reserved. No part of this publication may be reproduced, stored in a retrieval system or be transmitted in any form or by any means, electronic, mechanical, photocopying, recording, or otherwise, without the prior written permission of Weigl Educational Publishers Limited.

Cataloging-in-Publication Data

Dudley, Karen.
    Great African Americans in government / Karen Dudley.
        p.   cm. — (Outstanding African Americans)
    Includes index.
    Summary: Contains thirteen biographies of African Americans who have made outstanding contributions to the fields of government, politics, and diplomacy.
        ISBN 0-86505-820-2 (pbk.). — ISBN 0-86505-806-7 (library binding).
    1. Afro-American politicians—Biography—Juvenile literature. [1. Afro-Americans—Biography. 2. Politicians.] I. Title.   II. Series.
E185.615.D79 1997
973'.0496073'0922—dc20
[B]   96-35446
                                                              CIP
                                                              AC

Contents

Ralph Bunche

Personality Profile

Career: Diplomat and United Nations official.

Born: August 7, 1904, in Detroit, Michigan, to Fred and Olive Bunche.

Died: December 9, 1971, in New York City, New York.

Family: Married Ruth Harris, 1930. Had three children, Joan, Jane, and Ralph, Jr.

Education: B.A. (*summa cum laude*) in international relations, University of California, 1927; M.A. in government, Harvard University, 1928; Ph.D. in government, Harvard University, 1934.

Awards: Honorary L.L.D., Lincoln University, 1947; Nobel Peace Prize, 1950.

Growing Up

The grandson of a slave, Ralph was born in Detroit, Michigan. His father worked as a barber, and his mother was a musician. When Ralph was ten, his mother became ill. The family moved to Albuquerque, New Mexico, so his mother could recover in the drier climate. Two years later, in 1916, both of his parents died within a few months of each other.

Ralph was sent to live with his grandmother in Los Angeles, California. She was a strong woman who was an important influence in Ralph's life. She knew that her grandson was brilliant, and she urged him to work hard. He listened to her advice and graduated from high school with high honors in 1922.

Ralph went on to attend the University of California. He remembered his grandmother's advice and tried to be as successful as possible. In addition to studying, he played football, baseball, and was the star guard on three championship basketball teams. He did not have much money, so Ralph paid for his education by working part time as a janitor, a carpet layer, and an assistant in the political science department. He also won several athletic and academic scholarships. He graduated from university in 1927 with the highest honors. The people in Ralph's community raised one thousand dollars so he could continue his education. He headed for Harvard University in Massachusetts.

> *"[My grandmother was] the strongest woman I ever knew, even though she stood less than five feet high."*

Ralph was on the University of California's basketball team in 1925.

5

Developing Skills

"I have a bias against racial and religious bigotry. I have a bias against war, a bias for peace. I have a bias which leads me to believe that no problem of human relations is ever insoluble."

At the University of California, Ralph had become interested in world conflicts and the reasons behind them. At Harvard, he continued to pursue this interest. In 1928, Ralph received a Master's degree in government.

For four years after graduating, Ralph taught political science at Howard University in Washington, D.C. In 1932, he returned to Harvard to study for his doctorate degree. Ralph traveled throughout North and West Africa to gather information for his doctoral thesis. He returned to America and started writing. In 1934, his thesis won the Toppan Prize as the best essay in the social sciences.

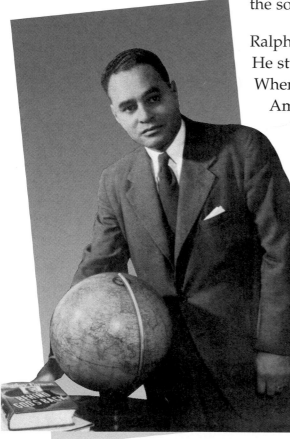

Ralph continued his education for two more years. He studied in Africa, England, and the United States. When he finished, he went on a trip around the world. Among the countries he visited were Japan, China, and the Philippines. He returned and taught at Howard until the outbreak of World War II.

In 1941, the United States entered the war. Ralph took a leave of absence from the university to help with the war effort. He worked with the Office of Strategic Services, a government department that gathered information about enemy activities. His travels before the war made him ideal for this job. He had learned a lot about Africa and the Far East. With this information, Ralph was able to advise the Joint Chiefs of Staff about some of the places American troops were stationed.

In 1944, Ralph worked for the State Department where he helped write the United Nations Charter, the rules and laws that govern the United Nations. The United Nations is an international organization that works to solve conflicts between countries. In 1946, Ralph went to work at the United Nations where he gained a reputation as a skilled, intelligent, and hard-working negotiator. He left this post in 1971 and died six months later.

George received the Gold Cross of Malta award from singer Marian Anderson in 1950.

Accomplishments

1934 Won the Toppan Prize for his doctoral thesis.

1937 Published his book *A World View of Race.*

1943-44 Chief of the African section of the Research and Analysis branch of the Office of Strategic Services (OSS).

1946 Appointed advisor to the United States delegation to the United Nations General Assembly in London, England. Started working as a negotiator for the United Nations.

1947 Named principal secretary to the United Nations Palestine Commission.

1948 Named acting mediator in the Palestine dispute.

1950 Won the Nobel Peace Prize.

1951 Named undersecretary at the United Nations. With this appointment, Ralph became the highest-ranking American at the United Nations.

1956 Helped establish a peace-keeping force in Egypt's Sinai Peninsula and the Gaza Strip. This force successfully kept peace in the area for eleven years.

1992 His 1937 account of his travels in Africa was published as *An African American in South Africa: The Travel Notes of Ralph J. Bunche.*

Overcoming Obstacles

At university, Ralph studied how people lived in Africa. In 1938, he traveled to South Africa to study at Cape Town University. He had trouble getting into the country. At that time, South Africa practiced apartheid, a policy of segregation which discriminated against blacks. The South African authorities were worried that Ralph might try to convince blacks to overthrow the government. Although Ralph did not agree with apartheid, he had to promise the authorities that he would not say anything against the government.

On this trip, Ralph bought a second-hand car and traveled throughout East and South Africa. He was held in high esteem by black Africans. In the villages, people greeted him with feasts and celebrations. Ralph was even made an honorary tribe member of the Kikuyu of Kenya.

Ralph signed autographs before speaking at the NAACP convention in 1962.

Ralph's reception was quite different when he returned to America. From 1938 to 1940, Ralph worked with the world-famous sociologist Gunnar Myrdal to research the relationship between blacks and whites in the United States. When Ralph and Gunnar traveled to the American South to gather information for their study, they were often run out of town. In two instances, they barely escaped lynching.

When he became a negotiator for the United Nations, Ralph always managed to stay calm in difficult situations. His life was in danger during the Palestine dispute of 1947. When the chief mediator was killed, Ralph took his place and negotiated for peace.

Ralph enjoyed time spent with his wife and three children.

Throughout the tense negotiations, Ralph kept his sense of humor. At one point in a difficult meeting, he took out some pottery and said, "I was going to give you these when we finished today, but now it looks as if I shall have to break them over your heads." He arranged a peace settlement for which he won the Nobel Peace Prize in 1950. He was the first black person to win the prize.

Ralph became known for his knowledge of international affairs and his negotiating skills. He was calm and kind towards others, but he could become angry if he saw anyone treated unfairly. When he died in 1971, he was described as an "American who belonged to all nations."

Special Interests

- Ralph was active in the American civil rights movement of the 1960s. He was also a member of the board of directors of the National Association for the Advancement of Colored People (NAACP).
- Ralph relaxed by reading novels, fishing, going to the theater, and playing pool.
- Ralph was a keen baseball fan. His favorite team was the Dodgers, and he closely followed Jackie Robinson's career.

Yvonne Braithwaite Burke

Personality Profile

Career: Lawyer and politician.

Born: October 5, 1932, in Los Angeles, California, to James and Lola Watson.

Family: Married Louis Braithwaite, 1957, (divorced, 1964); married William A. Burke, 1972. Has one daughter, Autumn Roxanne, and one stepdaughter, Christine.

Education: B.A., University of California, 1953; J.D., University of Southern California Law School, 1956.

Awards: Fellow, Institute of Politics, John F. Kennedy School of Government, Harvard University, 1971-72; Chubb Fellow, Yale University, 1972; Professional Achievement Award, UCLA, 1974, 1984; Future Leader of America, *Time* magazine, 1974; numerous awards from the Los Angeles City Council and the Los Angeles Board of Supervisors.

Growing Up

Yvonne was an only child. Her father was a janitor at the MGM movie studios, and her mother was a real estate agent. The couple had named their daughter Pearl Yvonne, but Yvonne dropped the name Pearl when she was still a child.

Growing up in a low-income housing area on the east side of Los Angeles, California, was not easy. Her parents tried to give Yvonne as many privileges as they could. They worked hard to save money so she could take lessons in dancing, piano, violin, and speech.

Yvonne worked hard at all her studies. Her elementary school principal was impressed by Yvonne's intelligence. He arranged to send her to a special school connected with the University of Southern California where she could get a better education.

Later, Yvonne attended the Manual Arts High School and became vice-president of the student body. She was an excellent student and won first prizes in local and state public-speaking contests. She had such high grades when she graduated that her father's union gave her a scholarship. Yvonne enrolled at the University of California. She helped pay for her education with part-time jobs in a clothing factory and at the college's library. In 1953, when she was twenty-one, Yvonne graduated with a bachelor's degree in political science.

> *"I always had a yard to play in and plenty of gardening."*

In 1972, Yvonne became a member of Congress.

Developing Skills

Yvonne became interested in law during her time at the University of California. After receiving her B.A., she enrolled at the University of Southern California School of Law. She still had very little money, so Yvonne modeled for *Ebony* magazine to help pay her expenses. She finished law school in 1956, graduating in the top third of her class.

At that time, there were few opportunities in law for black women. Many law firms refused to give them a chance. Yvonne knew she would have to help herself, so in 1956, she opened her own law practice.

"I want to be able to look back and say there are people whose lives are better because I served [in Congress]."

In 1964, Yvonne worked on the campaign to re-elect President Johnson. She became interested in politics and decided to run for the California General Assembly, one of the governing bodies of the state of California. In 1966, Yvonne became the first black woman ever to serve in the Assembly.

Yvonne was re-elected to the Assembly twice. During each term, she worked to improve the lives of low-income people. She voted for equal job opportunities for women, and child care for those who could not afford it. She wanted to increase funding for education. Yvonne also fought against racial discrimination.

In 1972, Yvonne decided to run for the U.S. Congress. She believed she would have more power there to improve the lives of low- and middle-income people.

In November 1972, Yvonne became the first black woman to represent the state of California in Congress. She fought hard for social change, supporting bills to protect the environment and guarantee equal rights for all citizens.

In 1979, Yvonne was sworn in as a Los Angeles County supervisor.

In 1978, Yvonne resigned from Congress, ran for state attorney general in California, but lost the election. The following year, Yvonne was appointed to the Los Angeles County Board of Supervisors, the governing body of Los Angeles County. She was appointed to take the place of a member who had died, and she was the first woman to serve on this board. She was defeated in the 1980 elections. Twelve years later, after a bitter election contest, she returned to the board. This time, Yvonne was the first African-American person to be elected to this position.

Accomplishments

1965 Appointed to the McCone Commission which investigated the causes of the Watts riots.

1966 Became first black woman elected to the California General Assembly.

1968, 1970 Re-elected to the California General Assembly.

1972 Became first black woman elected to represent California in Congress.

1973 Became first member of Congress to be granted maternity leave.

1979 Appointed to the Los Angeles County Board of Supervisors.

1984 Vice-chairperson of the Olympics Organizing Committee.

1992 Elected to the Los Angeles County Board of Supervisors.

Overcoming Obstacles

When Yvonne was studying at the special school connected to the University of California, she was well aware of racism. Sometimes, the other students teased her and made racist comments. When she grew older, she vowed to fight racism wherever she could. While she was in law school, Yvonne discovered that the campus women's law society refused to allow blacks or Jewish people to join. In response, she and two other students started a rival law society.

In 1965, African Americans who were tired of racism and poverty rioted in the Watts district of Los Angeles. When the riots were over, 34 people had been killed and almost 900 injured. Yvonne organized a legal team to defend the rioters. As part of the defense, Yvonne reported on the poor housing conditions in the area.

In 1973, Yvonne became the first member of Congress to be granted maternity leave.

In 1968, Yvonne was re-elected to the California General Assembly. It was a difficult year for her. Like many other African Americans, she was devastated when Martin Luther King, Jr., was assassinated on April 4, 1968. After Martin's death, Yvonne worked on Robert Kennedy's presidential campaign. When Robert was shot and killed, Yvonne's dreams of equal rights for African Americans were shattered. Later that summer, Yvonne's mother died. Despite these tragedies, Yvonne kept working. She was re-elected to the Assembly again in 1970.

At the 1972 Democratic Convention, Yvonne continued to fight against racism. She helped run a meeting to discuss changes to the convention rules. Some of these changes would allow minority groups more participation in the Democratic party. The discussion was loud and angry as people disagreed with one another over the changes. Throughout the eleven-hour meeting, Yvonne kept calm. The final vote gave minority groups more rights at conventions. Yvonne's professional manner during the convention helped her win a seat in Congress.

Yvonne has dedicated her life to public service. She has worked hard to improve conditions for blacks, for women, and for all underprivileged Americans. She hopes to see more African Americans in government and looks forward to the day when "we have a black governor, and, yes, a black president."

As a lawyer and politician, Yvonne has worked hard to help underprivileged people.

Special Interests

- Yvonne likes to relax by preparing gourmet meals. She especially likes French cooking.
- To keep in shape and reduce tension, Yvonne plays tennis and attends exercise classes.

Shirley Chisholm

Personality Profile

Career: Politician, educator, and author.

Born: November 30, 1924, in Brooklyn, New York, to Charles and Ruby St. Hill.

Family: Married Conrad Chisholm, (divorced, 1977); married Arthur Hardwick, Jr., 1977, (died, 1986).

Education: B.A. (*cum laude*), Brooklyn College; M.A., Columbia University.

Awards: Alumna of the Year Award, Brooklyn College, 1957; Sojourner Truth Award by the Association for the Study of Negro Life and History, 1969; Woman of the Year, Clairol, 1973; numerous honorary degrees.

Growing Up

Shirley's father worked in a burlap bag factory in Brooklyn, New York, and her mother was a seamstress and a domestic worker. The couple knew they would have trouble paying for their children's education. In 1927, when Shirley was three years old, she and her two sisters were sent to live on their grandmother's farm in Barbados so her parents could save some money.

For seven happy years, Shirley stayed at the farm. During this time, she attended an excellent elementary school. She learned to read when she was three-and-a-half years old and to write when she was four.

Shirley and her sisters returned to Brooklyn in 1934 in the middle of the Great Depression, a time when jobs and money were scarce. Shirley's parents had been unable to save much money, but they still managed to buy a piano and pay for lessons for the girls. Shirley's father taught his daughters about Marcus Garvey, an African American who wrote about black pride. Shirley's mother urged the girls to get the best education possible.

In Barbados, Shirley had finished grade five and was about to start grade six. When she began school in New York, she was put in grade three because she did not know enough about American history and geography. Within a year and a half, Shirley had caught up to the students in her age group. She continued to work hard during high school. When she graduated, she enrolled at Brooklyn College.

"Years later I would know what an important gift my parents had given me by seeing to it that I had my early education in the strict, traditional, British-style schools of Barbados. If I speak and write easily now, that early education is the main reason."

Developing Skills

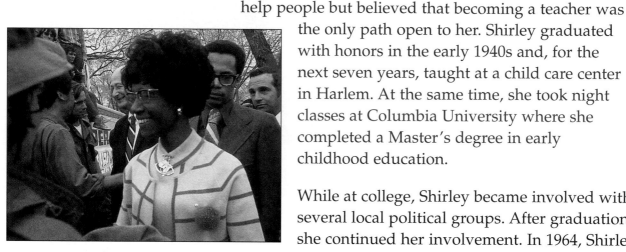

At Brooklyn College, Shirley studied sociology and won prizes in debating. Her professors and fellow students told her she should go into politics. Shirley felt this was an impossible dream because she was black and a woman. She wanted to help people but believed that becoming a teacher was the only path open to her. Shirley graduated with honors in the early 1940s and, for the next seven years, taught at a child care center in Harlem. At the same time, she took night classes at Columbia University where she completed a Master's degree in early childhood education.

While at college, Shirley became involved with several local political groups. After graduation, she continued her involvement. In 1964, Shirley was selected as the candidate for the Unity Democratic Club. She won the election and spent the next four years serving in the New York State Assembly.

During her time in the Assembly, Shirley gained a reputation as a fighter. She supported government-funded day-care centers. She fought to get unemployment insurance for domestic workers. She also brought in a bill to help disadvantaged students attend university.

When her term was over in 1968, Shirley was ready for a new challenge. The Supreme Court had formed a new congressional district in New York. A citizens' committee chose Shirley as their candidate because of her fighting spirit. She won the election and became the first African-American woman to be a member of the United States Congress.

"The next time a woman runs [for President], or a black, a Jew or anyone from a group that the country is 'not ready' to elect to its highest office, I believe he or she will be taken seriously from the start. The door is not open yet, but it is ajar."

Shirley was a member of Congress from 1969 until 1982. During this time, she fought to improve the standard of living for low-income people.

In 1983, Shirley began teaching political science and women's studies at Mount Holyoke College in Massachusetts. She was also a visiting scholar at Spelman College in Georgia. She stayed active in politics and worked on Jesse Jackson's presidential campaign in 1984 and again in 1988. Shirley has written two books about her life in politics.

In 1987, Shirley addressed a celebration at the Smithsonian Institution during Black History Month.

Accomplishments

1964 Elected to the New York State Assembly.

1969 Elected to the United States Congress.

1970 Wrote her first autobiography, *Unbought and Unbossed.* The book details her early life and her election to Congress.

1972 Ran for the Democratic party nomination for the United States presidency.

1973 Wrote her second autobiography, *The Good Fight.* The book examines her unsuccessful 1972 campaign for the Democratic nomination for the presidency.

1983 Became Purington Professor at Mount Holyoke College in Massachusetts.

1984 Co-founded the National Political Congress of Black Women.

Overcoming Obstacles

hen Shirley was growing up in Barbados, she was not aware of racism. Even in Brooklyn, the family lived in a quiet neighborhood where blacks and other minorities were accepted. In 1936, the family moved to Bedford-Stuyvesant in New York City. This community had more African-American people, but it also had more racial problems.

At home, Shirley's father spoke of black pride and unity. When Shirley began attending college, she heard others speak of the same thing. She developed a strong desire to help African Americans and other minorities rise above racism.

Shirley giving the black power salute with Adam Clayton Powell, Jr., in a 1969 parade in Harlem, New York.

In order to succeed in politics, Shirley had to overcome prejudice against her race, but she also had to fight prejudice against her gender. Many political organizations were run by men who did not want to give women any power. Shirley once said that being a woman turned out to be more of an obstacle for her than being black. Once she was elected to Congress, she made sure she hired other women for her staff.

Campaigning for Congress was not easy. Shirley did not have the money that most people had to run a campaign. She had to work extra hard. To make matters worse, in the middle of the campaign, Shirley was diagnosed with a tumor that her doctors had to operate on and remove immediately.

Shirley recovered quickly and headed back to the campaign. She beat her opponent by over 21,000 votes.

As a member of Congress, Shirley fought hard for social change. When her bills were defeated, she became frustrated. She began to believe that change had to begin at the top. With this in mind, Shirley decided to run for the Democratic presidential nomination in 1972. She was the first African American and the first woman to seek a presidential nomination.

Shirley held a press conference announcing her intention to run for president of the United States.

From the start, Shirley's campaign did not look hopeful. Many people were simply not ready for a black woman president. She failed to win support and lost the nomination. In spite of her loss, Shirley believes she opened the political door for other African Americans. In her book *The Good Fight* she wrote, "I ran because someone had to do it first....What I hope most is that now there will be others who will feel themselves as capable of running for high political office as any wealthy, good-looking, white male."

Special Interests

- Shirley earned the nickname Fighting Shirley Chisholm because of her strong opinions and beliefs.
- Shirley relaxes by reading and playing the piano.
- Shirley likes to do housework. She especially enjoys ironing because it gives her a quiet time for thinking.

Carol Moseley-Braun

Personality Profile

Career: Politician and lawyer.

Born: August 16, 1947, in Chicago, Illinois, to Joseph and Edna Moseley.

Family: Married Michael Braun, (divorced, 1986). Has one son, Matthew.

Education: B.A., University of Illinois, 1969; J.D., University of Chicago Law School, 1972.

Awards: Special Achievement Award, U.S. Department of Justice; Best Legislator Awards, Independent Voters of Illinois, 1978-88; Woman of the Year Award, Lu Palmer Foundation, 1980.

Growing Up

Carol was born, the oldest of four children, on August 16, 1947, in Chicago, Illinois. Her father was a police officer, and her mother was a medical technician. Her parents had a rocky relationship. When conflicts between the two adults flared up, young Carol often found herself acting as the protector of her brothers and sister.

In 1963, when Carol was sixteen, her parents divorced. Her mother took her four children and moved in with their grandmother. Their new neighborhood in Chicago was known as the "Bucket of Blood" because the people lived in terrible conditions. The poverty and despair that Carol saw made her want to help improve society.

Carol had always expected to go to college. When she graduated from high school, she immediately enrolled at the University of Illinois. Carol still dreamed of trying to improve society, so it seemed natural for her to study political science. After receiving her B.A. in 1969, she went on to attend the University of Chicago Law School. She received her law degree in 1972. The following year, she got a job as an assistant attorney in the United States Attorney's office under Jim Thompson, a man who later became the governor of Illinois.

"My parents were always philosophizing about how to bring about change. To me, people who didn't try to make the world a better place were strange."

Developing Skills

C arol first became involved in politics in 1968 when she volunteered to be a campaign worker for Harold Washington, a state representative. Harold later became the first African-American mayor of Chicago. Ten years later, after Carol had received her law degree, she entered politics herself and ran for a seat in the Illinois House of Representatives, the state's governing body. She won the seat and found her life's work in politics.

Carol speaking to the press about becoming the first African-American woman senator.

As a state representative, Carol fought to bring about change. She supported bills for gun control and greater funding for education. She fought for universal health care and other programs that helped women, minorities, and low-income people. Sometimes, she even fought against members of her own party if she did not agree with their positions. In 1983, she was selected as floor leader, an honor usually reserved for more senior representatives. In 1988, Carol became the Cook County Recorder of Deeds.

In the early 1990s, President George Bush nominated Clarence Thomas to serve on the Supreme Court. The United States Senate was responsible for reviewing Clarence's qualifications. Carol criticized his record as a judge and opposed his nomination. Then during the review, there were accusations that he had behaved inappropriately with a former worker, Anita Hill.

As Carol watched the review process on television, she became upset at the Senate's investigation. She believed that the senators, mainly wealthy, white men, were out of touch with other Americans. Carol began to think about running as a Democrat for a seat in the Senate. She believed the Senate needed people such as herself to change the way it operated.

Crowds cheer Carol at the Democratic National Convention in 1992.

Carol talked about her views on a local talk show. Many Illinois voters felt the same way as she did. They began writing and calling in their support. Carol even received a letter from a white man in a Republican county telling her to run for the Senate. In 1991, Carol announced that she would be running for a seat in the Senate. In 1992, she surprised political observers by winning the seat. She became the first African-American woman to become a U.S. senator.

Accomplishments

1973 Became assistant attorney in the United States Attorney's Office.

1978 Elected to Illinois House of Representatives.

1988 Elected Cook County Recorder of Deeds.

1992 Elected to United States Senate.

Overcoming Obstacles

"I am...a different kind of senator. I am an African American, a woman, a product of the working class...I come to the Senate as a symbol of hope and change."

Carol's involvement in civil rights began early in her life. As a high school student, she tried to break the color barrier by going into a whites-only restaurant. When the restaurant staff refused to serve her, Carol staged a one-woman sit-in. When Carol went to a whites-only beach, people threw stones at her. Carol did not lose heart and continued to work to end discrimination against African Americans. In 1968, she marched with Martin Luther King, Jr., in a civil rights demonstration in Chicago.

Governor Bill Clinton and Senator Al Gore support Carol's senate campaign in 1992.

As Carol grew older, she decided to fight for equal rights by entering politics. In the Illinois House of Representatives, the debates were often tense and angry. Carol wanted to win support for her beliefs, but she did not want to make enemies of her opponents. At the end of angry debates, Carol made a point of shaking hands with those who had disagreed with her. Sometimes she even presented them with a funny T-shirt or some colorful balloons.

Harold Washington, the mayor of Chicago, had named Carol floor leader in the House in 1983. Afterwards, the two had a falling out when Carol disagreed with some of Harold's policies. In 1986, when Carol tried to run for the position of lieutenant governor of Illinois, Harold blocked her attempt. It was a bad year for Carol. In addition to her political troubles, her marriage ended, her mother had a stroke, and her brother died from drug and alcohol abuse.

When Carol took over as Cook County Recorder of Deeds in 1988, the office was in a terrible mess. The recording system was outdated, and there were rumors of corruption among some of the staff. Within four years, Carol cleaned up the office. She established a code of ethics and brought in a computerized recording system. In the process, she gained a reputation as a skillful and efficient administrator.

When Carol announced that she wanted to run for the Senate, many people believed that she would never win. She was a little-known, African-American woman. Both her opponents were well-known, white men. She had little support from her fellow politicians and only a small amount of money to run her campaign. Her campaign manager left to undergo heart surgery, and at the same time, her deputy campaign manager left to become a judge. Despite these obstacles, Carol kept campaigning and won the seat.

After her election to Senate, Carol hoped the media attention around her would lessen.

Special Interests

- Religion is very important to Carol. She was raised a Roman Catholic but now describes herself as a born-again Christian. Her faith has helped her through the difficult times in her life.
- In her spare time, Carol likes to travel, look for antiques, and cook Italian food.

Adam Clayton Powell, Jr.

Personality Profile

Career: Member of Congress, civil rights activist, and minister.

Born: November 29, 1908, in New Haven, Connecticut, to Adam Clayton and Mattie Powell.

Died: April 4, 1972, in Miami, Florida.

Family: Married Isabel Washington, 1933, (divorced, 1944); married Hazel Scott, 1945, (divorced, 1960); married Yvette Diago, 1960, (divorced, 1965). Had three children, Preston, Adam Clayton III, and Adam Clayton IV.

Education: City College, New York; Colgate University, 1930; Union Theological Seminary; M.A., Columbia University, 1932.

Awards: Honorary degree, Shaw University, 1938; Artists and Scientists Award, American Committee of Jewish Writers, 1943; Dorie Miller and Meyer Levin Award, 1943; honorary degree from Virginia Union University, 1947; Knight of the Golden Cross, Ethiopia, 1954.

Growing Up

As the youngest in his family, Adam had a happy childhood. His father was a well-known pastor, and the family lived comfortably in New Haven, Connecticut. In 1922, when Adam was fourteen, his father became pastor at the Abyssinian Baptist Church in Harlem, New York.

Adam's father hoped his son would grow up to become a pastor. At elementary school, Adam's marks were good, and he studied hard. When he reached high school, however, his marks began to fall. He began to ignore his studies in favor of an active social life.

Adam's father convinced his son, after high school, to enroll at City College, New York. Adam attended classes but continued to enjoy the exciting night life in Harlem rather than concentrate on his studies. During Adam's first year at college, his only sister, Blanche, died of a burst appendix. Adam had been very close to his sister, and he was heartbroken by her death. He returned home, having failed his classes. That fall, Adam enrolled at Colgate University in upstate New York. This time, he concentrated on his studies and graduated in 1930.

Adam continued his education at Columbia University in New York City and received a Master's degree in religious studies in 1932. By this time, Adam had become the assistant minister at his father's church.

"My father said he built the church and I would interpret it. This I made up my mind to do."

Developing Skills

Many people suffered from poverty during the Great Depression of the 1930s. In Harlem, many African Americans were without work. When Adam saw the difficulties his people were experiencing, he vowed to help. He organized protests at companies that would not hire African Americans. Adam became known as a fighter for civil rights. He took his fight into print and wrote articles for the *New York Post* and the Harlem newspaper *Amsterdam.*

In 1937, Adam's father retired from the church, and Adam took his place as pastor. He often preached his views on the social conditions of African Americans. In 1941, he decided to run for the New York City Council. By sitting on council, Adam felt that he could represent his people's views and help the black community. He won the seat, becoming New York's first African-American city councillor.

Adam spent two years on city council. But when a new congressional district was formed in Harlem, Adam decided to run for the United States Congress. In his campaign, he promised to fight for fair employment and reduce taxes. He also wanted to make lynching a federal crime. In 1945, Adam was elected to Congress.

Adam addressing the National Negro Congress.

Adam had strong opinions and was very outspoken. For the first time, African Americans had a strong voice in Congress.

Adam worked hard to end discrimination against African Americans. In 1946, a bill came through Congress to provide money for a food program for school children. Adam attached an amendment, or change, to the bill. The change read that any state that excluded black children from the food program would not get any funding. The bill was passed.

Afterwards, Adam tried to add the same type of amendment to many other bills to hold back government money to states that practiced segregation. After a while, these changes became known in Congress as Powell amendments.

Adam campaigned to open more job opportunities for African Americans.

Accomplishments

1930 Became assistant pastor and business manager of the Abyssinian Baptist Church.

1935 Began writing a newspaper column called "Soap Box."

1937 Became pastor of the Abyssinian Baptist Church.

1941 Elected to New York City Council.

1942 Founded the newspaper *The People's Voice.*

1945 Elected to Congress.

1951-52 Delegate to the Parliamentary World Conference in London, England.

1961 Became chairperson of the House Committee on Education and Labor.

1961 Named delegate to the International Labor Organization Conference in Geneva, Switzerland.

Overcoming Obstacles

A dam's first real experience with racism happened at Colgate University. At the university, everybody thought that Adam was white because he had light skin and straight, dark hair. He allowed people to believe this. However, when Adam tried to join an all-white fraternity, the students checked his background and discovered that he was actually black. After that, the white students stayed away from him. The African-American students also ignored him. They felt he had tricked them and that he was ashamed of being black.

"Like no other Negro, except perhaps the late Malcolm X, Adam knew how to anger, to irritate and to cajole his white counterparts."
– Simeon Booker

In university, Adam had passed himself off as a white man because it allowed him a better social life. But Adam was proud of his heritage. When he became active in politics, he proved his pride by speaking out for black rights. Sometimes this got him in trouble with other politicians.

In 1945, President Truman's wife attended a tea hosted by the Daughters of the American Revolution (DAR). The DAR owned a performing hall that banned black performers. Adam told the president that his wife should not have attended because of the DAR's racist policies. The two men argued. As a result, Adam was never invited to the White House during President Truman's term in office.

As a member of Congress, Adam spoke out against other members when they used racial slurs. He tried to pass laws that would end segregation. In 1945, he published a book called *Marching Blacks*. In it, he urged African Americans living in the South to move up to the North where opportunities were better.

Adam giving a black power salute to the inmates of a New York prison.

In the late 1960s, Adam had many difficulties. He was accused of using tax payers' money illegally, and many people criticized his private life. He was often absent from Congress, even when important bills were passed. In 1967, his fellow members of Congress took away his seat. Adam took the case to the Supreme Court. In the meantime, a special election was held to fill his vacant seat. The Harlem voters re-elected Adam, and shortly after, the Supreme Court ruled in Adam's favor. Adam returned to Congress in 1969 but lost his seat in 1970. He was diagnosed with cancer in 1969 and died in 1972.

Special Interests

- Adam's aggressive approach in Congress towards civil rights issues earned him the nickname Mr. Civil Rights.
- Adam's favorite leisure activities included fishing, reading, and swimming.

Colin Powell

Personality Profile

Career: Career military officer, Chairman of the Joint Chiefs of Staff.

Born: April 5, 1937, in Harlem, New York, to Luther and Maud Ariel Powell.

Family: Married Alma Vivian Johnson, 1962. Has three children, Michael, Linda, and Annemarie.

Education: B.A., City College of New York, 1958; M.B.A., George Washington University, 1971; graduate of the National War College, 1976.

Awards: Purple Heart, 1963; Bronze Star, 1963; Legion of Merit Awards, 1969 and 1971; White House Fellow, 1971; Secretary's Award, Secretary of State, 1988; Spingarn Medal, National Association for the Advancement of Colored People (NAACP), 1991.

Growing Up

Many see Colin as a bridge-builder who united racial divisions and improved the military's image. Colin first learned these bridge-building skills as a child. He was born in New York City to Jamaican immigrants. The family lived in a multi-ethnic neighborhood, and Colin was used to listening to many different points of view.

"We came from a very structured home, and it gives you guidelines. You know where you're going."
– Marilyn Powell Berns, sister.

Colin's parents were hard workers. His father put in long hours as a shipping clerk, and his mother sewed clothes in a factory. They taught young Colin about the importance of hard work, discipline, and education. In 1945, when Colin was eight, he played hooky from school. He was caught because he misjudged the time and came home too early. For a long while after that, he was taken to school every morning and left at his classroom door.

While he was in high school, Colin worked at a store selling baby furniture. When he graduated in 1954, he entered the City College of New York to study geology. Colin also became a cadet in the Reserve Officers' Training Corps (ROTC). By the time Colin finished college, he held the top rank of cadet colonel. Colin then joined the army to "get out of New York, get a job and have some excitement." His ROTC achievements helped him to become a second lieutenant. At that time, he did not think his career was in the army.

Developing Skills

From an early age, Colin had an air of authority. On his sister's wedding day, the party's car was stopped for speeding. When the police officer approached the car, sixteen-year-old Colin snapped to attention, saluted him, and explained, "Wedding party, sir." They were allowed to go without a ticket.

This attitude of respect and authority helped Colin in his army career. His first assignment was in West Germany. After two years, Colin was assigned to a South Vietnamese infantry battalion. Colin was a brave soldier who received eleven medals, including two Purple Hearts, a Bronze Star, a Soldier's Medal, and the Legion of Merit.

Colin describing troop movements in Somalia during a 1991 press conference.

When the Vietnam War ended, Colin went to Washington, D.C., where he earned an M.B.A. from George Washington University. By this time, Colin was a major in the army. After he graduated from university, he accepted his first political position as a White House Fellow.

During the 1970s, Colin worked as a battalion commander in Korea. He was also commander of the Second Brigade of the 101st Airborne Division and an assistant to the deputy defense secretary. By 1979, Colin had been promoted to major general.

The 1980s saw Colin continue to rise in the military ranks. In 1989, he was awarded the nation's top military post, Chairman of the Joint Chiefs of Staff. He was the youngest man and the first African American ever to hold the position.

In August 1992, Iraq invaded Kuwait, starting the Gulf War. In his new role, Colin was responsible for planning all the land, air, and sea campaigns against Iraq. Colin had learned from his experiences in Vietnam and, together with General H. Norman Schwarzkopf, launched an attack against Iraq. Colin was hailed as a hero following the Gulf War.

Colin retired from the military in 1993. Some believed that he might run for president in 1996, but Colin decided against it. He said he wanted to spend more time with his family.

Colin and his wife at his 1993 retirement party.

Accomplishments

1976-77 Commander of the Second Brigade of the 101st Airborne Division in Fort Campbell, Kentucky.

1979-81 Senior military assistant to the deputy secretary of defense.

1983 Deputy commander at Fort Leavenworth, Kansas.

1983-86 Military assistant to the secretary of defense.

1986-87 Commanding general of the Fifth Corps in Frankfurt, West Germany.

1987-89 Served as assistant to the president for national security affairs.

1989 Named commander-in-chief of the U.S. Forces Command at Fort McPherson, Georgia. Later became Chairman of the Joint Chiefs of Staff in Washington, D.C.

1995 Wrote his autobiography, *My American Journey.*

"I never let my being black be a problem for me—if it was a problem, it was somebody else's problem, not mine."

An army officer spends a lot of time away from home, and Colin was no exception. He was sent to Vietnam only four months after his marriage to Alma Johnson whom he met on a blind date in 1961. When Colin left for Vietnam, Alma was pregnant with their first child. At that time, military families did not have much contact with soldiers on assignment. Colin did not even find out that he had a baby until his son was already three weeks old.

In addition to separations from his family, Colin had to face many other difficulties as a soldier. While he was on his first tour in Vietnam, Colin stepped on a Punji-stick, a trap made of poison-coated bamboo. He impaled his foot on one of the sharp stakes hidden underwater. He was given a Purple Heart for his injury.

During his second tour in Vietnam, Colin was injured in a helicopter crash. He managed to pull fellow soldiers out of the flames and wreckage and was awarded the Soldier's Medal for bravery.

Colin at a 1995 book signing in California.

Throughout his childhood, Colin was not really aware of racism. The first time he experienced racial discrimination was during his assignment at Fort Benning in the American South. The military people were not prejudiced against him, but whenever he and his white comrades went to a bar, his friends had to force the bartenders to serve him.

Despite this experience, Colin has always said that being black was never a problem for him. During the Gulf War, black leaders criticized Colin and the army for sending such a large number of African Americans to the Gulf. They believed that he was doing what the whites in power wanted. Colin refused to apologize for the army. He said that the military offers blacks more opportunities than most other American institutions.

Colin is now seen as a role model for young blacks. During his military career, he always made a special effort to meet the African Americans under his command. He has praised the work of black activists who "suffered and sacrificed to create the conditions and set the stage for me."

General Colin Powell in a parade welcoming troops returning from the Persian Gulf.

Special Interests

- Colin loves meeting young people. He encourages them to stay in school and work hard.
- He enjoys watching old movies with his wife and prefers eating a peanut butter and jelly sandwich at home to dining out in restaurants.
- Colin's favorite hobby is fixing his vintage Volvo automobile.

L. Douglas Wilder

Personality Profile

Career: Politician.

Born: January 17, 1931, in Richmond, Virginia, to Robert and Beulah Wilder.

Family: Married Eunice Montgomery, 1950s, (divorced, 1978). Has three children, Loren, Lynn, and Lawrence, Jr.

Education: B.S., Virginia Union University, 1952; J.D., Howard University, 1959.

Awards: Bronze Star, 1953; Spingarn Medal, National Association for the Advancement of Colored People (NAACP), 1990.

Growing Up

Douglas had a long family history with racism. His grandparents had been slaves who were sold to separate owners after their wedding. Douglas's grandfather needed a special pass to visit his wife. The only time they could see each other was on Sunday. The two were reunited after slavery was abolished in 1863.

Born on January 17, 1931, Douglas was raised in an all-black neighborhood in Richmond, Virginia. His parents did not have a lot of money, but the family always had enough to eat. Douglas's father was an insurance salesman who was strict with his children. Douglas's mother worked as a maid. She believed in the importance of a good education and made Douglas learn a new word every day.

Young Douglas did well in school. In his spare time, he earned extra money for his family by shining shoes, washing windows, running an elevator, and delivering papers. While attending high school, he worked as a waiter in Richmond's whites-only clubs and hotels.

After graduating from high school, Douglas wanted to join the navy, but his mother refused to give her permission. He enrolled at Virginia Union College, an all-black school where he majored in chemistry. He decided to study law, but before he could enroll in law school, Douglas was drafted into the army and sent to fight in the Korean War in 1951.

"[While I was growing up] it was stressed that however things are, they can be better if you make them better. We were never told there were limitations."

Developing Skills

When Douglas returned from the war, he got a job as a chemist at the state medical examiner's office. He worked there for a few years, running tests on blood for alcohol content. But Douglas never forgot his dream of becoming a lawyer. In 1956, he quit his job and enrolled at Howard University's Law School in Washington, D.C. When he graduated in 1959, he went back to Richmond to open his own law practice.

Douglas specialized in criminal law. Over the next ten years, he took on many difficult cases. He gained a reputation for being an excellent lawyer. In 1969, Douglas decided to try his luck in politics. With the support of a few other lawyers, he ran for a seat in the state Senate, one of the governing bodies of the state of Virginia. It was a three-way race. Douglas was up against two white men. He won the election, becoming the first African American ever elected to the Virginia Senate.

Douglas supported many bills to find solutions to community problems.

From the beginning, Douglas was an outspoken senator. In his first speech, he attacked the Senate for its racist policies. He proposed a bill to change the state song, "Carry Me Back to Old Virginia." The song portrayed slavery as a condition loved by both master and slave. Douglas believed the song was insulting to blacks. The other senators disagreed, and his bill was never passed.

During his sixteen years as a state senator, Douglas worked hard on many different committees. He supported bills dealing with fair housing and labor rights. By 1985, he was rated among the five most important members of the state Senate. That same year, he ran for lieutenant governor and won the election.

In 1989, Douglas was the first African American to be elected governor of a state.

In his speeches, Douglas urged African Americans to work together to solve the problems in their communities. His popularity soared. When he announced that he would run for governor, many flocked to his support. In 1989, Douglas was elected the first African-American governor of Virginia.

Accomplishments

1953 Won a Bronze Star for heroism at Pork Chop Hill in Korea.

1959 Opened his own law practice in Richmond, Virginia.

1969 Elected to Virginia state Senate where he served until 1986.

1985 Elected lieutenant-governor of Virginia.

1989 Elected governor of Virginia.

1991 Announced his intention to run for the 1992 Democratic presidential nomination. He dropped out of the race a few months later.

1995 Started a radio talk show called *The Doug Wilder Show*. The show ran from January to August, 1995.

Overcoming Obstacles

"[Working as a waiter in the whites-only hotels and clubs,] racial jokes were told in your presence. It was like you were an invisible man."

By far the biggest obstacle Douglas had to overcome was racism. He first became aware of discrimination against blacks when his mother took him on a city bus when he was four or five years old. At that time, blacks were allowed to sit only in the back of buses. When Douglas grew older and started working at whites-only clubs and hotels, racism was even more obvious. Many of the white patrons made racist jokes as Douglas served them. He often became very upset at their comments and found it hard to ignore his anger.

Douglas was sworn in as governor of Virginia on January 13, 1990.

In a battle during the Korean War, Douglas fought his way through enemy fire to rescue his wounded comrades. He was awarded the Bronze Star for his bravery. When he got back to Virginia after the war, he applied for a job as a chemist at the medical examiner's office but was told that the job was not open anymore. They suggested that he go to work as a cook. Douglas eventually got the job as a chemist, but he never forgot the humiliation of not being considered for the job just because he was black.

When Douglas decided to go to law school, he had to leave the state. At that time, Virginia did not allow blacks to attend law school. When he graduated, he returned to practice law in Virginia, but found it difficult at first to make a living. Sometimes he had to wash and wax his office floors himself between seeing clients.

When Douglas decided to run for lieutenant governor, many thought he had no chance of winning. At this time, only nineteen percent of the voters in Virginia were black. In order to win, Douglas had to convince white voters to elect him. He rented a station wagon and began campaigning. For two months, he drove across the state, making speeches and attending hundreds of meetings. On election day, his efforts paid off. Douglas was elected lieutenant governor. He earned a reputation for hard work which helped him win the election for governor in 1989. He served as governor until 1994.

In 1995, Douglas hosted a two-hour morning radio show. Despite the show's popularity, Douglas cancelled it the same year because it took up too much of his time. He left to write a book about the historical roots of today's problems.

Douglas at a 1990 convention of the National Urban League.

Special Interests

- Douglas likes to relax by playing pool and listening to baroque music.
- Douglas is a member of the Masons, a men's society. He is a thirty-third degree Mason, which means he has special recognition of his outstanding service to the community.

Julian Bond

*"If people remember me,
I hope it's not for what I've
already done, but for what
I'm still going to do."*

J ulian was the only African-American student at George School, a Quaker boarding school in Bucks County, Pennsylvania. He had never experienced racism as a child, and at school, the white students accepted him as equal. However, when he wore his school jacket to Philadelphia on a date with his white girlfriend, the dean told him he should not have worn the jacket. Julian thought this was because the school disapproved of his being seen in public with a white girl. He felt as if he had been slapped across the face. From that moment, he became aware of racism.

In 1957, when he was seventeen, Julian enrolled at Morehouse College in Atlanta, Georgia, where he took classes in English and philosophy. At that time, students were beginning to organize sit-ins to protest against discrimination against blacks. Julian joined the sit-ins and started writing poems about racial injustice.

While Julian was a student, he helped found the Committee on Appeal for Human Rights (COHAR), a student organization fighting for civil rights. In 1960, Martin Luther King, Jr., invited all the student civil rights groups, including COHAR, to form one large organization called the Student Nonviolent Coordinating Committee (SNCC). In 1961, halfway through his senior year at Morehouse, Julian left college to work for the *Atlanta Inquirer*, a black newspaper he and other students founded. He also became the communications director of the SNCC.

By 1964, some of the SNCC's members wanted to change the organization's policy of non-violence. Julian began to worry about his involvement with the group. He was afraid his young family might be in danger from angry whites if the SNCC pursued more violent action. He decided to go into politics instead.

Personality Profile

Career: Civil rights activist and politician.

Born: January 14, 1940, in Nashville, Tennessee, to Horace and Julia Bond.

Education: Morehouse College, 1971.

Awards: Honorary degrees from numerous institutions, including Dalhousie University, University of Oregon, Syracuse University, Tuskegee Institute, Howard University, and Lincoln University; honorary trustee of the Institute of Applied Politics.

In 1965, Julian won a seat in the Georgia House of Representatives, the governing body of the state. Before he could take his seat, however, he became caught up in a controversy. In early 1966, the SNCC had protested against the United States's involvement in the Vietnam War. Julian had publicly agreed with the SNCC's position. He had also expressed his support for people who avoided the draft. The Georgia House of Representatives labeled Julian a traitor and voted against admitting him.

Eager to take his place in the House, Julian ran for vacant seats in two more elections. He won both times, but the House members still refused to let him sit. Julian took his case to court. The case eventually reached the Supreme Court which ruled in his favor. Finally, in early 1967, he was sworn in as a member of the Georgia House of Representatives.

In 1968, Julian gained a lot of support at the Democratic party's national convention. He became the first African-American candidate for the U.S. vice-presidency. However, Julian withdrew from the race. He was only twenty-eight, which was too young for the job. The Constitution states that vice presidents must be at least thirty-five years old.

Julian successfully ran for the Georgia Senate in 1974 and held the seat until 1987. Since then, he has kept busy lecturing, writing, teaching, and narrating documentaries for the PBS and HBO television networks.

Accomplishments

1960 Co-founded the Committee on Appeal for Human Rights.

1961 Became communications director for the Student Nonviolent Coordinating Committee.

1966 Elected to the Georgia House of Representatives.

1968 Named candidate for the U.S. vice-presidency.

1974 Named president of the Atlanta branch of the National Association for the Advancement of Colored People (NAACP).

1974 Elected member of the Georgia Senate.

1988 Became visiting professor at various institutions including Drexel University, Harvard University, and the University of Virginia.

David Dinkins

D avid attended Trenton High School in New Jersey where most of the students were white. The few black students were not allowed even to use the school's swimming pool. Despite the racism at his school, David became class president, defeating a white classmate. This was his first taste of political success.

After graduating in 1945, David tried to join the marines but was told the "black quota" was filled. He was drafted into the army but was later transferred to the Marine Corps. When he was released from service, he enrolled at Howard University in Washington, D.C., to study mathematics.

Despite the racism at his school, David became class president.

During the summers, David returned to New Jersey to work in a factory. Unhappy with the racism he saw there, David complained to the New Jersey civil rights commission. His efforts resulted in the desegregation of the washrooms at the factory and of a local bar which had refused to serve blacks.

David graduated from Howard with honors. He was awarded a math fellowship to Rutgers University but dropped out when he became restless. David became a successful insurance salesman. In 1953, he married Joyce Burroughs. Joyce's father was active in law and politics. At his father-in-law's urging, he enrolled at Brooklyn Law School.

After he graduated, David became active in local politics. At first, he worked on other people's campaigns, hanging posters and talking to undecided voters. After a while, his political ambitions grew. With the support of his friends, David was elected to the New York State Assembly.

David served in the State Assembly for only one year, from 1965 to 1966. In 1966, his district was redrawn, and he decided not to run again for office. David continued to be active in politics, but at the local level.

In 1973, David helped Abraham Beame's campaign to become mayor of New York. After he won, Abraham named David deputy mayor for planning as a reward for his hard work.

Personality Profile

Career: Politician and mayor of New York City.

Born: July 10, 1927, in Trenton, New Jersey, to William and Sally Dinkins.

Education: B.S., Howard University, 1950; J.D., Brooklyn Law School, 1956.

Awards: Named Pioneer of Excellence, World Institute of Black Communications, 1986; Righteous Man Award, New York Board of Rabbis, 1986; Distinguished Service Award, Federation of Negro Civil Service Organizations, 1986.

Before David could officially accept the position, however, people discovered that he had not paid taxes for four years. Although David paid back the taxes with interest, he lost his position as deputy mayor. He was named city clerk, a job in which his main duty was to sign marriage certificates.

In 1989, David decided to run for mayor of New York City. During his campaign, a white woman was attacked and beaten by black youths in Central Park. The entire city was ready to explode with racial tension after the crime. David urged people to remain calm and gained a reputation as a peacemaker. On election day, David defeated his opponent and became the first African-American mayor of New York City.

In 1992, a black man, Rodney King, was brutally beaten by white police officers in Los Angeles, California. When the officers were found not guilty of the crime, many people expected riots to break out in cities across the country. Again David kept racial tensions calm in New York. Although his reputation as a peacemaker grew, many did not care for his leadership decisions. In the 1993 elections for mayor, David lost.

Accomplishments

1956 Became partner in the law firm Dyett and Phipps.

1965 Elected to New York State Assembly.

1967 Named district leader of the New York State Democratic party.

1975 Appointed city clerk for New York City.

1986 Elected Manhattan borough president.

1989 Elected mayor of New York City.

W. Wilson Goode

Wilson was the first of his family to receive a college education.

Wilson was born in a small shack in the farming community of Seabord, North Carolina. His parents were sharecroppers who could not afford indoor plumbing or electricity for their home. In 1958, when Wilson was fifteen, the family moved to Philadelphia, Pennsylvania, hoping to find a better life.

Wilson was an honors student in high school. After he graduated, he enrolled at Morgan State University. He was the first of his family to receive a college education. Wilson received his B.A. in 1961. From 1962 until 1963, he went on a tour of duty with the United States Army, rising to the rank of captain and receiving a commendation medal.

After his time in the army, Wilson held a number of jobs. He worked as a probation officer, a building maintenance supervisor, and an insurance adjuster. He then attended the University of Pennsylvania's Wharton School where he received a master's degree in public administration.

In 1969, Wilson became the executive director of the Philadelphia Council for Community Advancement, an organization that helps improve low-income neighborhoods. Wilson's work with the council earned him a lot of publicity.

Wilson's public service skills were further recognized when he was appointed head of the Pennsylvania Public Utility Commission, a body that governs the state's utility rates. When disaster struck the Three Mile Island nuclear power station in 1979, Wilson investigated the accident. He made sure that everyone in the area had a safe and dependable source of power.

In 1980, the mayor of Philadelphia named Wilson the managing director of the city. He worked hard in his new job, often working seven days a week. He held meetings about problems in the city and even rode on garbage trucks during neighborhood cleanup projects. Many hoped Wilson would run for mayor in the 1983 elections. He did not disappoint his supporters. On election day, Wilson became the first African American mayor of Philadelphia.

Personality Profile

Career: Politician and mayor of Philadelphia.

Born: August 19, 1938, outside Seabord, North Carolina, to Albert and Rozella Goode.

Education: B.A., Morgan State University, 1961; M.P.A., Wharton School, 1968.

Awards: Commendation medal for meritorious service, United States Army, 1963; Outstanding Young Leader of the Year, Philadelphia Jaycees, 1972; numerous honorary degrees from schools including the University of Pennsylvania and Temple University.

When Wilson took office in 1984, he had many plans to help the city. He wanted to reduce racial tension and unemployment. He wanted to clean up neighborhoods and improve housing conditions. Wilson became very popular during this time. Democratic senator Walter Mondale even considered him for a running mate in the 1984 presidential elections.

Things became difficult for Wilson in 1985. Members of MOVE, a radical back-to-nature group, took over a run-down house in Philadelphia. For fifteen months, the police tried to evict them. Wilson finally gave the police permission to use force. A gunfight resulted, and the police dropped an explosive on the roof of the house. Eleven people were killed and many houses in the area were destroyed. Wilson accepted responsibility for the incident, but his reputation never recovered.

In 1987, Wilson was re-elected mayor by a narrow margin. In his second term of office, he developed heart troubles and had to cut down on his hectic work schedule. When his term was over in 1992, Wilson retired from politics.

Accomplishments

1969 Became executive director of the Philadelphia Council for Community Advancement.

1978 Appointed head of the Pennsylvania Public Utility Commission.

1980 Named managing director of the city of Philadelphia.

1983, 1987 Elected mayor of Philadelphia.

1992 Published *In Goode Faith*, the story of his life in politics.

Patricia Harris

Because of her excellent marks in high school, Patricia was offered scholarships from five colleges. She chose Howard University in Washington, D.C., where she graduated with the highest honors in 1945. She was also elected into Phi Beta Kappa, an organization of top college students. While at Howard, Patricia became involved in the civil rights movement. She joined in sit-ins and other protests and worked as vice-chair for the student branch of the National Association for the Advancement of Colored People (NAACP).

After her time at Howard, Patricia went on to study industrial relations at the University of Chicago. In 1949, she returned to Washington and worked for social organizations. For a while, she was an assistant director for the American Council of Human Rights. In 1957, she enrolled in law school.

While at Howard, Patricia became involved in the civil rights movement.

Graduating at the top of her class in 1960, Patricia went to work as a researcher for the Department of Justice. In 1961, she began part-time teaching at Howard University Law School. Two years later, Patricia's job was made full time. She was one of just two women professors on the faculty.

Patricia took a leave of absence from the school when President Johnson chose her to be the U.S. ambassador to Luxembourg in 1965. She was the first African-American woman to represent the United States in another country.

Leaving the diplomatic service, Patricia returned to Howard University in 1969. She became dean of the university's law school, the first time a black woman had ever held the position. Due to disagreements with other faculty members, Patricia resigned from the position after only one month. She stayed in Washington and joined a law firm where she worked for a number of years as a corporate lawyer. She also served on the boards of several corporations, including IBM and the Chase Manhattan Bank. Patricia believed that big businesses could work together to fight racial discrimination.

Personality Profile

Career: Lawyer, ambassador, and U.S. cabinet secretary.

Born: May 31, 1924, in Mattoon, Illinois, to Bert and Hildren Roberts.

Died: March 23, 1985, in Washington, D.C.

Education: A.B. (*summa cum laude*), Howard University, 1945; University of Chicago, 1946-9; American University, 1949; George Washington University Law School, 1960.

Awards: Alumni Achievement Award, George Washington University, 1965; Distinguished Achievement Award, Howard University, 1966; Order of Oaken Crown, 1967.

Patricia became the first African-American woman to serve in a president's cabinet when President Carter named her Secretary of Housing and Urban Development (HUD) in 1977. As Secretary of HUD, Patricia worked for equality in housing and employment. She was a woman of humble beginnings, and she knew what it was like to struggle against poverty and discrimination. She understood the problems faced by low-income and minority groups.

In 1982, Patricia ran for mayor of Washington, D.C, but lost. The following year, she became a law professor at George Washington University where she taught until her death in 1985.

Accomplishments

1961 Became lecturer and associate dean of students at Howard University Law School.

1963 Co-chair of the National Women's Committee for Civil Rights, an organization of over 100 women's groups.

1965 Appointed as American ambassador to Luxembourg.

1969 Named dean of Howard University Law School.

1977 Appointed U.S. Secretary of Housing and Urban Development.

1980 Appointed U.S. Secretary of the Department of Health, Education, and Welfare.

1983 Became law professor at George Washington University.

Sharon Pratt Kelly

Sharon grew up with the belief that women should be strong and intelligent and should speak their minds freely.

hen Sharon was only four, her mother died. Sharon's father often told her and her sister about their mother's strength of spirit. Sharon grew up with the belief that women should be strong and intelligent and should speak their minds freely. Even as a child, Sharon was determined. She would not use training wheels on her first bicycle, despite many falls and badly scraped knees.

Sharon was raised in a supportive all-black neighborhood in Washington, D.C. During her early school years, she was not a very good student. She preferred baseball to school work. However, when she reached high school, she decided to work harder. She graduated as class president with straight A's on her report card.

After high school, Sharon studied political science at Howard University in Washington, D.C., and graduated with her B.A. in 1961. She continued at the university's law school and earned a law degree in 1968.

Sharon married the year before she received her law degree. For a while, she stayed at home, raising her two daughters and supporting her husband's career in local politics. At that time, she never thought of entering politics herself.

In 1971, Sharon began working as a lawyer in her father's law firm. She fought for the rights of children and young people. At the same time, she taught at the Antioch School of Law in Washington. She left both positions in 1976 to work as a lawyer at the Potomac Electric Power Company. In 1983, she was the first African-American woman to become a vice-president in the company.

At the same time that Sharon started work at the power company, she also became involved in politics. She worked for the Democratic party, and in 1985, she became its first woman treasurer. Her political goals involved plans to improve the economy. Sharon also wanted to develop ways in which minority groups could have more power in government.

Personality Profile

Career: Lawyer and mayor of Washington, D.C.

Born: January 30, 1944, in Washington, D.C., to Carlisle and Mildred Pratt.

Education: B.A., Howard University, 1965; J.D., Howard University Law School, 1968.

Awards: Falk Fellowship, Howard University, 1962-65; Harvard University Cooperative Scholarship, 1964.

By the mid-1980s, the city of Washington was in trouble. It had a huge debt and there were rumors of corruption in the city council. To make things worse, Washington had such a high murder rate that people called the city the murder capital of the United States. Sharon hated hearing about the problems in her home town and decided to do something. In 1989, she announced that she would run for mayor.

Sharon had to work hard during her campaign. She did not have the money to hire a large campaign staff, and she could not afford to run advertisements on television. Few voters even knew who she was. Sharon campaigned steadily, promising to clean up the corruption in city hall if she was elected. Her slogan was "clean house with a shovel, not a broom." The voters listened to her. In 1990, she became the first African-American woman to be elected mayor of a major American city. In 1994, Sharon lost the election to former mayor Marion Barry.

Accomplishments

1971 Became associate at the law firm Pratt and Queen.

1976 Became associate general counsel for the Potomac Electric Power Company (PEPCO).

1977 Elected Democratic national committee woman for the District of Columbia.

1979 Became director of the office of consumer affairs at PEPCO.

1983 Named vice-president of PEPCO.

1985 Elected treasurer of the Democratic party.

1990 Elected mayor of Washington, D.C.

Constance Baker Motley

Constance's parents had immigrated to New Haven, Connecticut, from the Caribbean before she was born. New Haven had only a small African-American population, but Constance learned about black history and culture at her church.

When she was fifteen, Constance first experienced racism. She and some friends were turned away from a roller-skating rink because they were black. Constance became interested in civil rights and began reading more about black history. She thought about how she could change things and decided to become a civil rights lawyer.

Constance and a group of friends were turned away from a roller-skating rink because they were black.

Constance graduated from high school with good marks, but her parents did not have enough money to send her to college. A local, white business person heard Constance speaking about civil rights at a community center. He was so impressed that he offered to pay her college costs. Constance enrolled at Fisk University in Tennessee, graduating in 1943 with a major in economics. Afterwards, she attended New York City's Columbia Law School as one of very few women at the school at the time.

Since her first experience with racism, Constance had wanted to do something to help other African Americans. In her final year of law school, she began to work as a law clerk for Thurgood Marshall, a top lawyer for the National Association for the Advancement of Colored People (NAACP).

In 1949, Constance became a trial lawyer for the NAACP Legal Defense and Educational Fund. As part of the NAACP legal team, Constance worked on many ground-breaking civil rights cases. She argued against segregation and defended people who had taken part in civil rights demonstrations. Among her clients were Martin Luther King, Jr., and Ralph Abernathy. Ten of her civil rights cases made it to the Supreme Court. She won nine of them.

Personality Profile

Career: Lawyer, politician, and federal judge.

Born: September 14, 1921, in New Haven, Connecticut, to Willoughby and Rachel Baker.

Education: B.A., New York University, 1943; LL.B., Columbia Law School, 1946.

Awards: Elizabeth Blackwell Award, Hobart and William Smith College, 1965; Columbia Law School Medal for Excellence, 1987; New York State Bar Association Gold Medal Award, 1988; honorary degrees from numerous universities and colleges, including Yale University, 1987; Georgetown School of Law and Princeton University, 1989; Tulane University and the University of Connecticut, 1990.

As Constance gained respect for her hard work, other opportunities opened up for her. In 1964, she was the first African-American woman elected to the New York State Senate, one of the governing bodies of the state. In 1965, she was elected president of the Borough of Manhattan.

In both positions, Constance pressed for equal rights for African Americans. In the Senate, she worked on solving employment, housing, and education problems. In the borough, she designed a plan to improve conditions in Harlem and other low-income areas. By 1966, her work for civil rights was recognized by President Johnson. He appointed Constance judge for the Southern District of New York. Many southern senators and a few federal judges objected because they did not want an African-American woman in a federal court. Finally, the U.S. Senate approved the appointment. Twelve years later, Constance became chief judge of her court, a position she held until 1986.

Accomplishments

1948 Admitted to the New York state bar.

1949 Appointed assistant counsel for the NAACP Legal Defense and Educational Fund.

1961 Appointed associate counsel for the NAACP Legal Defense and Educational Fund.

1964 Elected to New York State Senate.

1965 Elected president of the Borough of Manhattan.

1966 Appointed to the U.S. District Court for the Southern District of New York.

1982 Became chief judge of the U.S. District Court for the Southern District of New York.

Index

2 3 4 5 6 7 8 9 0 Printed in the United States 6 5 4 3 2 1